KIDNEY STONES

Four One Act Comedies

by
Frederick Stroppel

SAMUEL FRENCH, INC.

Other Samuel French titles by FREDERICK STROPPEL

ACTOR!

A CHANCE MEETING

DO OVER

DOMESTIC VIOLENCE

FORTUNE'S FOOLS

A GOOD MAN

KIDNEY STONES

MAMET WOMAN

MORNING COFFEE

PACKAGE DEAL

SINGLE AND PROUD

Please consult our BASIC CATALOGUE for complete details.

KIDNEY STONES

Four One Act Comedies

by
Frederick Stroppel

SAMUEL FRENCH, INC.
45 West 52th Street   7623 Sunset Boulevard
NEW YORK 10010   HOLLYWOOD 90046
LONDON   *TORONTO*   ATHENS OHIO

Copyright © 2004 by Frederick Stroppel

ALL RIGHTS RESERVED

CAUTION: Professionals and amateurs are hereby warned that ITCH, SMOKE-OUT, CRASHING THE GATE, HARVEST TIME is subject to a royalty. It is fully protected under the copyright laws of the United States of America, the British Commonwealth, including Canada, and all other countries of the Copyright Union. All rights, including professional, amateur, motion picture, recitation, lecturing, public reading, radio broadcasting, television and the rights of translation into foreign languages are strictly reserved. In its present form the play is dedicated to the reading public only.

The amateur live stage performance rights to ITCH, SMOKE-OUT, CRASHING THE GATE, HARVEST TIME are controlled exclusively by Samuel French, Inc., and royalty arrangements and licenses must be secured well in advance of presentation. PLEASE NOTE that amateur royalty fees are set upon application in accordance with your producing circumstances. When applying for a royalty quotation and license please give us the number of performances intended, dates of production, your seating capacity and admission fee. Royalties are payable one week before the opening performance of the play to Samuel French, Inc., at 45 W. 25th Street, New York, NY 10010; or at 7623 Sunset Blvd., Hollywood, CA 90046, or to Samuel French (Canada), Ltd., 100 Lombard Street, Lower Level, Toronto, Ontario, Canada M5C 1M3.

Royalty of the required amount must be paid whether the play is presented for charity or gain and whether or not admission is charged.

Stock royalty quoted upon application to Samuel French, Inc.

For all other rights than those stipulated above, apply to Samuel French, Inc.

Particular emphasis is laid on the question of amateur or professional readings, permission and terms for which must be secured in writing from Samuel French, Inc.

Copying from this book in whole or in part is strictly forbidden by law, and the right of performance is not transferable.

Whenever the play is produced the following notice must appear on all programs, printing and advertising for the play: "Produced by special arrangement with Samuel French, Inc."

Due authorship credit must be given on all programs, printing and advertising for the play.

ISBN 0 573603251   Printed in U.S.A.   #12990

No one shall commit or authorize any act or omission by which the copyright of, or the right to copyright, this play may be impaired.

No one shall make any changes in this play for the purpose of production.

Publication of this play does not imply availability for performance. Both amateurs and professionals considering a production are strongly advised in their own interests to apply to Samuel French, Inc., for written permission before starting rehearsals, advertising, or booking a theatre.

No part of this book may be reproduced, stored in a retrieval system, or transmitted in any form, by any means, now known or yet to be invented, including mechanical, electronic, photocopying, recording, videotaping, or otherwise, without the prior written permission of the publisher.

IMPORTANT BILLING AND CREDIT REQUIREMENTS

All producers of **ITCH, SMOKE-OUT, CRASHING THE GATE, HARVEST TIME** must give credit to the Author of the Play in all programs distributed in connection with performances of the Play, and in all instances in which the title of the Play appears for the purposes of advertising, publicizing or otherwise exploiting the Play and /or a production. The name of the Author must appear on a separate line on which no other name appears, immediately following the title and must appear in size of type not less than fifty percent of the size of the title type.

KIDNEY STONES
was presented at the
Nuyorican Poets Café
in New York City in January 2003.
The evening was directed by Frederick Stroppel,
and the cast was as follows:

ITCH

RALPH.........................Brian Corrigan
CHIFFON....................Maria Fernanda

SMOKE-OUT

FAITH..........................Cindy Keiter
CRYSTAL....................Heather Male

CRASHING THE GATE

DOOLEY......................Kevin Kash
SARAH........................Heather Male

HARVEST TIME

BILLY..........................Kevin Kash
MIKE...........................Brian Corrigan
AMY............................Cindy Keiter

HARVEST TIME was originally presented at the Nuyorican Poets Café in June 2002, with the following cast:

BILLY..........................Kevin Kash
MIKE...........................Peter Plano
AMY............................Heather Male

TABLE OF CONTENTS

ITCH	9
SMOKE-OUT	17
CRASHING THE GATE	31
HARVEST TIME	47

ITCH

(A Motel Room. CHIFFON, a hooker, ENTERS with RALPH..)

RALPH. *(Looking around.)*...Wow. What a great motel room.
CHIFFON. It's all right. Has a nice view of the reservoir.
RALPH. And what is your name, my dear?
CHIFFON. Chiffon.
RALPH. Chiffon? That's a lovely name!
CHIFFON. Yeah.
RALPH. My name is Ralph.
CHIFFON. *(Bored.)* Whatever.
RALPH. Have you been doing this a long time? You look so fresh-faced and vibrant...
CHIFFON. Look - can we get started? Because, you know, I'm on the clock right now. You go one minute over the hour, you're paying double.
RALPH. Duly noted.
CHIFFON. Plus I get a break every twenty minutes, regardless of your level of stimulation. It's a union thing.
RALPH. I'm in the Writers Guild myself, so I completely sympathize.
CHIFFON. And I don't do any weird shit. By which I mean to say, if I do any weird shit, it's an extra three hundred.
RALPH. Sounds more than fair.
CHIFFON. And I can't stand on my head, so don't even ask.
RALPH. I'm not planning on making any extraordinary demands. I don't think you'll even break a sweat.
CHIFFON. Yeah, we'll see. *(Beat.)* So - you gonna take your clothes off?
RALPH. No, I don't think so.
CHIFFON. You want me to take my clothes off?
RALPH. Not necessary.
CHIFFON. Do you need to take a pill or something?
RALPH. No, I'm all set.

(Beat.)

CHIFFON. Well, what's it gonna be, tiger? The suspense is fucking killing me.
RALPH. Actually - I have this itch in the middle of my back, and I can't reach it...?
CHIFFON. Uh huh.
RALPH. It's one of those itches, it's really deep, it feels like it's under

the skin, absolutely maddening. Right in the center, just beyond my fingertips, taunting, teasing, tantalizing me. I need someone to scratch it.
CHIFFON. You want me to scratch your back?
RALPH. Yes, please.
CHIFFON. That's what you want?
RALPH. Would you mind?
CHIFFON. That's why you hired me.
RALPH. It's driving me crazy.
CHIFFON. *(Shrugs.)* Whatever. *(RALPH sits on the bed, and CHIFFON starts scratching his back.)* Like this?
RALPH. Yeah...a little higher...and to the left...Ahh!
CHIFFON. Is that too hard?
RALPH. No, that's...oh, yes...!
CHIFFON. *(Sexy voice.)* You like that, huh?
RALPH. Oh, yeah...Oh, yeah...
CHIFFON. That feels good, doesn't it?
RALPH. Wonderful, won-der-ful...
CHIFFON. You want more, don't you?
RALPH. Yes, more, more...!

(Beat.)

CHIFFON. You're sure you don't want me to take my shirt off, at least? It's included in the price.
RALPH. No, this is fine...a little nail action, please...Yeah... Ooo..
CHIFFON. Or I could talk dirty. I learned a lot of foreign curses from Op Sail.
RALPH. No, no...A little more to the center...Ah...Mmmm...
CHIFFON. I got my other hand free, you know; I can just reach down there and...
RALPH. Please, no distractions. Just - Ahh!...Ahhhhh! Ecstasy!

(Beat, as she continues scratching.)

CHIFFON. *(Getting bored.)* I think I'm gonna put on some music...
RALPH. No, don't stop. Keep going!

(Beat.)

CHIFFON. Some weather we're having, huh...?

KIDNEY STONES

RALPH. Don't talk! Just scratch!

(Beat.)

CHIFFON. They say El Nino is coming back...
RALPH. Will you please be quiet! Please!

(Beat.)

CHIFFON. *(Finally stops scratching.)* This is too fucking boring for me.
RALPH. Excuse me?
CHIFFON. You bring me all the way out here to scratch your back? You don't think I have better things to do?
RALPH. Hey, I'm paying you, am I not?
CHIFFON. That's beside the point. I'm a professional. I've spent years in the service industry polishing my craft, and I have a certain reputation. You think I'm someone you can just pull in off the street?
RALPH. *(Bewildered.)* Yes.
CHIFFON. Hey, don't break my balls. I have a long list of satisfied customers, I've produced orgasms in all forty-eight contiguous states, and FYI, my pelvis is double-jointed. Incredible, but true. I'm a superstar in my field. So when you take up my valuable time for a fucking backrub, it's not only insulting, it's a mockery of everything that I hold sacred.
RALPH. Isn't it your vocation to make people happy?
CHIFFON. There are limits, pal. I don't mind screwing you or giving you a blow job, but I'm not going to humiliate myself.
RALPH. I'll pay you extra. You can have my watch.
CHIFFON. You're not getting it. I'm a sexual performer! This is not sex! This is something you can do with your wife!
RALPH. *(Quietly.)* No, it isn't. *(Sighs.)* My wife used to scratch my back. Not anymore.
CHIFFON. She's dead?
RALPH. Far from it - she's quite the lively one. She just doesn't want to touch me. She finds me - repulsive.
CHIFFON. Well, she's got a point.
RALPH. Oh, when we were newlyweds, she would scratch my back anywhere, anytime. She took pleasure in it. I would sometimes invent itches, just to give her the chance to employ those elegant fingernails of hers. Oh! - but they were long and shapely, like talons, with just a hint of the mandarin about them. Like your nails, my dear. Yes, they remind me of hers.

KIDNEY STONES

CHIFFON. *(Self-consciously pleased.)* Do they?
RALPH. But that was in the early days. With time the wild passions faded, the scratch sessions were fewer and farther between. And then one day I came home and she had gotten - a manicure.
CHIFFON. *(Gasps.)* No!
RALPH. *(Nods.)* Every digit, trimmed to the bone. Well, the handwriting was on the wall. One of the great joys of marriage is the option of having any itch scratched with scrupulousness and affection, no questions asked. Take that away, and what's left? Naturally, I sought relief elsewhere. A man has itches, they can't be controlled.
CHIFFON. You could have used a backscratcher.
RALPH. I also could have rubbed my back up against a pine tree. But I'm a human being! I want to be touched! Sure, it's easy for you, you can walk into any bar or OTB parlor in the world and say "Would you please scratch my itch?", and the boys would be lining up for blocks. But where can I turn? If I approach a stranger on the street and ask to have my back scratched, can I expect anything more than revulsion and ridicule? No, I have to pay a professional sex-monger for a simple act of civility! Do you realize how emasculating that is? How disenfranchising? How crippling to the soul?
CHIFFON. All right, all right, I'll scratch your fucking back. Just stop whining, will ya?
RALPH. It's a hard, hard thing to itch alone. *(She resumes scratching him.)* Ohhh!...Ahhhh!
CHIFFON. If your wife won't scratch your back, why don't you leave her?
RALPH. I should, I really should. But she makes fantastic potato pancakes.
CHIFFON. Man, you have some weird fucking priorities.
RALPH. You're missing the spot.
CHIFFON. Right here?
RALPH. No, higher...
CHIFFON. Here?
RALPH. No...You had it before.
CHIFFON. This is exactly the same spot.
RALPH. No, it isn't.
CHIFFON. Yes it is.
RALPH. Don't you think I know where my own itch is?
CHIFFON. Well, your itch must have moved.
RALPH. Just scratch a littler higher...Now that's too high! Lower...Okay, now, harder...! Scratch harder...! Aiiee, not that hard!

KIDNEY STONES

CHIFFON. *(Walks away.)* All right, that's it!
RALPH. What...?
CHIFFON. *(Gathers up her things.)* No wonder your wife won't touch you. You're a pain in the ass.
RALPH. Where are you going? Don't stop...
CHIFFON, I don't need to put up with this bullshit. I'm not married to you.
RALPH. No, please! I'll be good!
CHIFFON. Sure, I know your type. "Higher! Lower! This way! That way! Counter-clockwise!" Never satisfied. I'll bet you terrorized that poor woman with your freaky epidermal demands, you needy bastard.
RALPH. That's not true. She loved it. I'm a lovable person.
CHIFFON. You're a monster. I don't even want your money. That reminds me, where's my money?
RALPH. Here, here. Take it all. Just don't leave me.
CHIFFON. I'm supposed to stay here, so I can spend the next hour scratching the dead skin off your spine? Scratch *this*, bozo. Oh, and guess what? *(Wiggles her fingers.)* They're not real. *(She pulls off a nail.)* Press-ons, baby!
RALPH. Oh, Jesus, no!
CHIFFON. That's right. I was faking it. I didn't feel a thing.
RALPH. I don't believe you! I won't!

(He starts to weep.)

CHIFFON. You're pathetic. So long, Itchy.
RALPH. No! Don't go! I'll fuck you! I will!
CHIFFON. Too late now.

(CHIFFON EXITS.)

RALPH. Please, Chiffon! Scratch my back! Scratch my back...!

(He crumples on the floor, distraught, as LIGHTS OUT.)

KIDNEY STONES

COSTUME PLOT

RALPH
Herringbone or tweed blazer
White shirt
Khaki pants
Brown/black shoes

CHIFFON
Black leather coat
Tight blouse or pull-over
Thigh-high black boots
Fishnet stockings
Short shorts
Press-on fingernails

SMOKE OUT

(The alcove outside an office building. CRYSTAL, early 20's, is wrapped in a black leather coat, smoking a cigarette. FAITH, mid-to-late40's, comes out of the building, also in a coat. She stakes out the opposite side of the alcove, and lights up a cigarette.)

FAITH. *(Nods to CRYSTAL.)* Hello.
CRYSTAL. Hi.

(Both take nice long drags on their cigarettes.)

FAITH. This is ridiculous, isn't it? Standing out in the freezing cold. America.
CRYSTAL. Some bullshit.
FAITH. Secondary smoke...! We never had secondary smoke years ago. Now, suddenly...And how do they know? Where's the proof?
CRYSTAL. Who cares anyway?
FAITH. Well...I care. I don't think anyone should have to die unnecessarily. But I think it's a shame, some big shot somewhere gets an idea in his head, and the rest of us have to suffer. The problem is, the people who complain about smoke? - they don't smoke! They don't even have a stake in it. Think about that. And these are the same people, you know, who were doing drugs and God knows what all those years, and now they say *smoking* is bad? I mean, I smoked marijuana myself when I was a dumb kid, but I never did heroin. People who do heroin or acid, they get spaced out and they walk right off the roof. That's not dangerous? That's not bad for the environment?
CRYSTAL. Heroin is overrated anyway.

(Beat.)

FAITH. I'm Faith.
CRYSTAL. Crystal.
FAITH. Crystal - that's pretty. Are you with Ludlow, Ludlow and Pierce?
CRYSTAL. Yeah.
FAITH. I work for Mr. Ludlow. The second Ludlow, the son. Not the wheelchair.
CRYSTAL. I'm with Mr. Pierce.
FAITH. Oh, he's cute.
CRYSTAL. He's okay.
FAITH. He always has a clean neck. I like a nice clean neck. You're his secretary?

CRYSTAL. I'm a secretary for one of his associates. Mrs. Gindi.

FAITH. *(Nods.)* Oh, Florence Gindi, yes, I've dealt with her. She's a bitch. I mean, I shouldn't say that, you might find her very nice. I just know that in my dealings with her, I've found her very unhelpful. And snide. But I could be always catching her on a bad day.

CRYSTAL. No, she's a bitch.

FAITH. I thought so. I wouldn't want to work for her.

CRYSTAL. *(Shrugs.)* Gotta work for somebody.

FAITH. I refuse to work for unpleasant people. Mr. Ludlow is a real gentleman. Very patrician. You know what that means, 'patrician'? *(CRYSTAL shakes her head.)* It's like..Roman. You know how those old Romans were. High-toned. British accents. *(Beat; she snickers.)* An associate? That's what she calls herself? I don't think so. She's a glorified secretary. She does the same work I do. She just makes more money. *(Beat.)* I'll bet things are crazy in your office right now?

CRYSTAL. I guess a little.

FAITH. Things are crazy up there. Things are not good. I half-expect someone to land right out here on the sidewalk one of these days. Right here in front of us. Splat! It won't be me, though. I don't bother with stress. I keep my life stress-free. They want to go nuts, that's their business. I learned a long time ago, you get involved in things, you get *involved* in things. So I don't.

CRYSTAL. I don't even know what's going on half the time.

FAITH. That's the best way to be.

(They smoke.)

FAITH. You know, people can't even smoke in the theaters anymore. Not even the actors. I went to a play somewhere off-Broadway, like in the meat district, my friend's son was in it; he's... *(Flutters her hand, enough said.)*...And they were all *pretend*-smoking. They were holding cigarettes, but they weren't lit, and then they were putting them out when they weren't even burning. Smashing up perfectly good cigarettes, and then taking out new ones! So ridiculous, you can't even smoke in the meat district.

CRYSTAL. Yeah, that sucks.

(They smoke.)

FAITH. *(Points across the street.)* See, that's a shame. That building - it's going to ruin our whole view. Mr. Ludlow is furious. But that's Donald

KIDNEY STONES

Trump. He sticks his buildings everywhere, he doesn't care. They're just like big, big...
    CRYSTAL. Big penises.

(FAITH is momentarily shocked, and then starts to laugh.)

    FAITH. You're right. That's exactly what they are. Do I need that? Do I need to have Donald Trump's ding-a-ling in my face every day? You know, I just like to come out here and smoke and look at New Jersey. And soon that'll be gone. No one cares about ordinary working people.
    CRYSTAL. I met Donald Trump once.
    FAITH. Really?
    CRYSTAL. In Atlantic City. I touched him.

(FAITH waits, but CRYSTAL offers nothing more. Long beat.)

    FAITH. So what did you do for New Year's? Party all night? You young kids. *(Sighs.)* We stayed home, just had a few friends over. I don't like having too many people at my house, because if you want to go to sleep, you have to wait for them all to leave. And especially on New Year's, everybody thinks they have to celebrate. Not me. Just another day to me. We went very simple. Appetizers, a little cheese platter. One bottle of champagne, that's all you really need. And salsa. When I was a kid we didn't have salsa. Or hummus, either, but hummus, yuck - I told Jack, no hummus, please, it's New Year's Eve. So we had chips and salsa, and cocktail franks, and shrimp, and a big chocolate-chip cookie, as big as a pizza. It was delicious. And we watched the ball come down, and the confetti, and we banged on our pots and pans...it was very nice. I was in bed by one. That's a perfect New Year's, for me.
    CRYSTAL. I was giving some guy a blow job.
    FAITH. Oh?
    CRYSTAL. Yeah, some guy. He was playing with my head all night, flirting and shit, telling stupid jokes - that's the fucking Internet, everyone knows a million jokes now, and none of them are funny. We wound up in somebody's bedroom, some kid's, all these Pokemons and Smurfs on the wall, and he wanted to get laid - that was his big dream, getting laid at twelve midnight - but I said no, just a blow job, take it or leave it. He took it. After all, I'm not gonna take my clothes off in some stranger's house. I'm not that drunk.

(Beat.)

KIDNEY STONES

FAITH. Yes, I hate those computers, too. They're really taking over.

CRYSTAL. We had regular sex later, but not at midnight. Turns out he works for American Express, and he's gonna get me an interview there. So it was worth the extra effort.

FAITH. *(Concurs.)* It's a good company. Anyway, I'm always glad when the New Year comes around. We can all make a fresh start. Put all that old stuff to rest. You know - the past. I'm so sick of the past. Like the Holocaust. That's all you ever hear about, the Holocaust, the Holocaust, the Holocaust! You know what? It was last *century*! Get over it!

CRYSTAL. My grandfather was in the Holocaust.

FAITH. He was? Oh, I'm so sorry. That's awful. That's terrible.

CRYSTAL. Yeah. I don't know if he was killed or anything. I just know he was in it.

FAITH. Well - if he was in it, he was probably killed, don't you think?

CRYSTAL. He might have been a Nazi. I'm not sure. I know he was involved somehow.

FAITH. There were probably a lot of good Nazis. You just don't hear about them. Could I borrow a ciggie?

CRYSTAL. Sure.

FAITH. *(Takes a cigarette.)* I usually smoke just one, but I'm in no rush to go back up there. It's so crazy. *(Lights up.)* Every year I try to give up smoking during that Great American Smoke-Out thing. But, you know, that's a big gimmick by the tobacco companies. They want people to stop smoking so they can say their profits are off, and they can raise their prices - but then, when everyone starts smoking again, do you think the prices go back down? No way. That's why I keep smoking. Because I don't want them making money.

CRYSTAL. I smoke to keep my weight down. It's a health thing.

FAITH. But you look so thin.

CRYSTAL. Because I smoke. I'm also bulimic.

FAITH. That's not good, honey.

CRYSTAL. No, but it works. Otherwise, I'd be a fucking horse. I don't want to ever be fat. I don't want my mother's ass.

FAITH. Well - who does?

CRYSTAL. Men don't want you if you're fat.

FAITH. Who cares what men want?

CRYSTAL. Fuck men.

(They smoke.)

KIDNEY STONES

FAITH. Are you one of those goths, by any chance? Because I notice you have the whole black thing going. The clothes, and the eyes...

CRYSTAL. I'm just into black. I *could* be a goth, but I don't go for trends. I prefer to be unique.

FAITH. My daughter wants to be a goth, but I think she's too young. Fourteen. She should be a candy-striper or something. Do you like that music?

CRYSTAL. It's okay.

FAITH. So depressing. I used to listen to the Carpenters. They were always happy. "Top of the world, looking down on creation..." *She* was anorexic.

CRYSTAL. I'm not anorexic; I'm bulimic.

FAITH. I'm just saying, you can have an eating disorder and still be happy.

CRYSTAL. I'm happy enough.

(They smoke.)

FAITH. It's so crazy up there. Everyone's acting paranoid. Not Mr. Ludlow, but the rest of them...Fighting with each other, and you see people crying, and then nobody's talking...

CRYSTAL. What's it all about? Is it about something?

FAITH. I don't know. Some big merger didn't merge, because somebody dropped the ball, or fell asleep at the switch, or something like that, and now they all want to sue each other. Makes no sense to me. If I were running this company...if we were in charge...

CRYSTAL. Yeah, tell me about it.

FAITH. So much stress...! Not a cheerful workplace. Maybe I should go to American Express. Call your friend; *I'll* give him a blow job. *(Giggles nervously.)* I'm only joking. I don't even like saying that word. It's so distasteful, somebody putting their ding-a-ling in your mouth...! To me, it's like hummus.

CRYSTAL. Well, I always say, it beats getting fucked in the ass.

FAITH. Yes, that's certainly something to keep in mind.

(They smoke.)

FAITH. So - Donald Trump? He's sexy, isn't he?

CRYSTAL. Not in real life. With that fat porky face - he reminds me of, who was that famous fat guy? - Nero.

FAITH. *(Chuckles.)* Well - I wouldn't mind being his fiddle. *(CRYSTAL*

registers blank. FAITH explains.) Because Nero invented the fiddle.
CRYSTAL. He did?
FAITH. Oh, yes - he was famous for that. And then he burned Rome. So that's why I'm saying, if Donald Trump played the fiddle, I wouldn't mind being his...you know. It's a play on words.

(Beat.)

CRYSTAL. I wonder who invented blow jobs?
FAITH. *(Ponders.)* Oh - I know they go way back. Even when I was a little girl, you heard about them.
CRYSTAL. Some man, I'm sure. They've got nothing else to think about, you know? Probably tried every hole they could find. "No, it doesn't fit in her ear...Doesn't fit up her nose...Hey! Here we go! And there's a tongue in there and everything...!" Pigs.
FAITH. You think about men too much.
CRYSTAL. I don't think about them. They're just always in the fucking way.
FAITH. Not all men are pigs. Mr. Ludlow is so good to his wife. I've seen some of the things he's bought here. He treats her like she was the Queen of Sheba or something. And she's *not*.

(Beat.)

CRYSTAL. Are you having like a thing with Mr. Ludlow?
FAITH. A thing? Me?
CRYSTAL. Because you mention him a lot. Mr. Ludlow, Mr. Ludlow, Mr. Ludlow...
FAITH. He's my boss.
CRYSTAL. I know, but...You sure?
FAITH. Excuse me - I'm a married woman. I take my marriage vows very seriously.
CRYSTAL. Well, he's doing something with somebody, right? Because that's what we hear.
FAITH. You hear what? What do you hear?
CRYSTAL. That's the word on our floor. Somebody in his office, some hot-ass babe - yeah, so it wouldn't be you, sorry - Some woman who was in accounting, and then she got bumped upstairs because, I don't know, her tits were too big for accounting.

KIDNEY STONES

FAITH. Not - Natasha?
CRYSTAL. Is she Ukrainian? 'Cause I hear the two of them go out and do this Ukrainian folk-dancing every Tuesday night. That's like their thing. She's got braided hair, and these big sausage arms... *(FAITH shakes her head.)* Hey, it's what I hear.
FAITH. Well, the people on your floor have very little to keep them busy, I guess. No wonder the firm is falling apart. I'll bet your Mrs. Gindi started that rumor. Back-biting bitch - I know her game. *(Beat.)* And you should watch yourself, missy, spreading stories like that. You don't know who I am. I could be anybody. I could have you fired.
CRYSTAL. For what?
FAITH. For spreading stories.
CRYSTAL. You can't fire someone for telling the truth.
FAITH. Of course you can. You're devaluing the stock. It's very unprofessional.
CRYSTAL. I'm not the one who's sleeping with my boss. *That's* unprofessional.
FAITH. I'm not sleeping with anyone!
CRYSTAL. Who said you were? Jesus Christ.

(Beat.)

FAITH. You know, you'd better get back upstairs, you've been out here a long time.
CRYSTAL. Excuse me, I don't work for you.
FAITH. Oh, you're getting an attitude now? Listen, I was your age once, I used to think I was hot shit, too. Guess what? I wasn't. *(An irritated sigh.)* I didn't come out here to have an argument. I just want to smoke.
CRYSTAL. Go ahead, who's stopping you?

(They smoke.)

FAITH. I don't like *stress*. *(Beat.)* Did anyone see them together?
CRYSTAL. I don't know.
FAITH. Well, you're the one shooting off your mouth -
CRYSTAL. *(Crossly.)* You know, I'm over here, you're over there - okay?
FAITH. Fine. Suddenly she has nothing to say. *(Beat.)* Even if he is doing something - and I don't believe he is, because why would he be interested in someone like that, she's so *vulgar*, with the ugly jewelry and the big mouth, and with the company in the shape it's in...But even if he is, well, if it makes

KIDNEY STONES

him happy, I mean for God's sake, with the money he's got, if you can't be happy...We all make mistakes. You're gonna make more than your share, honey, I can see that right off. So don't be so smug.
    CRYSTAL. I thought you were just gonna smoke and shut up.
    FAITH. Don't tell me to shut up. I'll shut up when I'm good and ready. *(FAITH notices her cigarette is finished. She rifles through her bag, in vain.)* Do you have any more cigarettes? *(CRYSTAL takes out her cigarette pack, looks inside.)*
    CRYSTAL. Yeah.

(Beat.)

    FAITH. May I have one?
    CRYSTAL. No.

(She put the cigarettes away.)

    FAITH. No? No? You have a whole pack of cigarettes, and you're purposely not giving me one? That's childish, you know. Do you know you're being childish? *(CRYSTAL cooly blows a cloud of smoke in her face.)* All right, whatever. Keep your precious cigarettes. Smoke them all, every last one, develop a nice juicy cancer for yourself. Then we'll see who cares how skinny you are, won't we? Won't we? *(Beat.)* It's too goddamn cold out here for me...!

(FAITH heads back toward the building. But she stops dead at the door, agitated.)

    FAITH. Oh, Jesus...Oh, my Lord. They're in the lobby.
    CRYSTAL. Who?
    FAITH. Mr. Ludlow, and...

(CRYSTAL goes to the door, looks into the lobby.)

    FAITH. Look at them - they're *pawing* each other. They're like *animals*...!
    CRYSTAL. Fucking sausage arms.

(FAITH turns away. She can't hide her distress. CRYSTAL calmly hands her a cigarette.)

KIDNEY STONES

FAITH. Thank you. *(FAITH tries to light the cigarette.)* Look at this - my hand is shaking. Because I'm shocked. I can't believe he would do that. Right there in the lobby - that is so...!
CRYSTAL. *(She lights FAITH'S cigarette.)* He's a pig. C'est la vie.

(Beat, as FAITH takes a long draw on her cigarette.)

FAITH. I guess I owe you an apology.
CRYSTAL. *(Shrugs it off.)* Ahhh...
FAITH. No, no, you were right, I was wrong. I don't know why I wasted my time defending him, the old goat.
CRYSTAL. Hey, you got a little crush on him - it happens.
FAITH. I'm forty years old, I don't have crushes.
CRYSTAL. *(Skeptical.)* You're forty?
FAITH. I *admire* him, I respect him as my boss, but I don't...Look, he's married and he has a girlfriend. Not much room for me, is there? I don't want to even get involved. It's not worth it. But I can't believe that Natasha. What a scheming little...whore, you'll excuse the expression. There's no other word.
CRYSTAL. *(Shrugs.)* People screw their bosses. Makes life interesting.
FAITH. It's not the way I was brought up. Anyway, I have a husband of my own. That's more than enough. You're not married, are you?
CRYSTAL. Fuck no.
FAITH. Good for you. Marriage...it never ends. It just never ends. *(Beat.)* Did you ever let anybody do that? Stick it up your whatsit?
CRYSTAL. No. There was one guy who tried, but he really didn't have the reach.
FAITH. I could never...! My mother once told me, you have to keep something for yourself. *(Looks into the lobby.)* Are they gone? They're gone. I should go back upstairs.
CRYSTAL. Yeah, I guess me too. Back to the fucking grind.
FAITH. Although why I should worry, I don't know. The company's falling apart, he's off folk-dancing...Nobody cares anymore. It's very sad. Oh, well. *(Puts out her cigarette.)* Maybe we should go up separately. Otherwise people will think we were talking.
CRYSTAL. Whatever.
FAITH. But we should do this again. There are so few of us left. Smokers.
CRYSTAL. That's for fucking sure.

(They shake hands.)

FAITH. So nice meeting you, Crystal.
CRYSTAL. Yeah, you too.
FAITH. Faith.
CRYSTAL. Peace.
FAITH. No, my name is Faith.
CRYSTAL. I know.
FAITH. Oh. I thought you forgot.
CRYSTAL. No.
FAITH. Oh. Okay, then.

(FAITH heads into the building.CRYSTAL shrugs, finishes her cigarette.)

KIDNEY STONES

COSTUME PLOT

CRYSTAL
Black leather hull-length coat
Black jeans
Black scarf
Black boots
Black eye-shadow
Black lipstick

FAITH
Beige full-length winter coat
Pantsuit, or slacks and blouse
Scarf
Gloves

PROPERTY PLOT

Cigarettes
Cigarette lighter
Ashtray stands

KIDNEY STONES

CRASHING THE GATE

(A motel room. DOOLEY is sitting in a chair, flipping cards into a wastebasket. He misses, most of the time. There are cards littered all over the floor. A cryptic knock on the door, DOOLEY doesn't respond. After a beat, another cryptic knock..)

DOOLEY. *(Annoyed.)* Oh, just come in. The door's open.

(SARAH ENTERS, carrying plastic grocery bags.)

SARAH. What the fuck, Dooley? You leave the door open? Suppose I'm FBI or something?
DOOLEY. I knew it was you. You did the knock.
SARAH. I did the knock because I thought the door was locked. If I was FBI I could have just walked in the door.
DOOLEY. If you were FBI, you'd break down the fucking door whether it was locked or not. Come on. All this stupid espionage shit...
SARAH. You're such a fuck-up.
DOOLEY. Oh, and you're not.

(DOOLEY resumes flipping cards into the basket. SARAH puts down her bags on the table..)

SARAH. Did they call?
DOOLEY. No Ma'am.
SARAH. Shit. What are they waiting for? I want to *do* this.
DOOLEY. The brain trust. Your boy Jasper.
SARAH. He's not my boy.
DOOLEY. Yeah, right.

(SARAH watches DOOLEY flip cards, and observes his high failure rate..)

SARAH. You really good at this game, aren't you?
DOOLEY. I'm not trying. What'd you get?

(SARAH upends the bag on the dresser top.)

SARAH. All kinds of junk. I got Crunchy Cheetos, and chocolate milk, and a couple of apples, and a Del Monte fruit cocktail, and Twizzlers...
DOOLEY. Hostess cupcakes?
SARAH. They didn't have cupcakes.

DOOLEY. Fuck!

SARAH. I got you Devil Dogs.

DOOLEY. I hate Devil Dogs. They're so fucking dry. Man, this is one fucked-up operation.

SARAH. *(Holds up plastic-wrapped sandwiches.)* And some pre-made sandwiches. This is turkey something, and this is tuna.

DOOLEY. Pre-made tuna? Great. Where's the beer?

SARAH. I told you no beer. I don't want you bombed if we have to go out.

DOOLEY. I'm not gonna get bombed on a fucking six-pack.

SARAH. Well, even so.

DOOLEY. Even so, what? You're not my fucking mother. I have to drink what, fucking gatorade?

SARAH. I'd like to maintain a little professionalism, if that's at all possible.

DOOLEY. Hey - I'm a total professional. Alcohol doesn't affect me. And even if it did, if I want to get all drunk and shit-faced, that's my decision, isn't it? I mean, this is the very thing we're fighting against, right? Fucking government interference. You're doing the same thing here - abridging my fucking rights. Fucking Russia all over again.

SARAH. *(Holds up devil dogs.)* So you don't want them?

DOOLEY, I'll take them. But they're dry as shit. Just going on record with that.

(DOOLEY grabs some snacks and sits on the bed to eat. SARAH paces.)

SARAH. I can't believe nobody called. I thought sure today...

DOOLEY. We're gonna miss our window, you know. The longer we wait, the better chance our cover's gonna get blown. Shit, we could have aced this deal a week ago if they hadn't kept dicking around. Your buddy Jasper, the big mastermind...What kind of name is that for a revolutionary? Jasper?

SARAH. What kind of name is Dooley?

DOOLEY. Dooley was my mother's maiden name, so don't break my balls.

SARAH. If it weren't for Jasper, this operation would still be at Square One. He made all the calls, arranged everything...

DOOLEY. Oh, like this flea-bag motel? Big points for that.

SARAH. A motel is a motel.

DOOLEY. Come on. This is a grade-A dump. One vending machine - no menus for take-out - the ice machine is all the way at the other end of the

KIDNEY STONES

parking lot - you can't get porno on the TV. You can't even get World Wrestling.
SARAH. We're not on vacation, Dooley.
DOOLEY. We're the operatives, Sarah. You're supposed to take care of your operatives. Keep up the morale. Would it kill them to send us a pizza once in a while? Buy us a little gift? Just show some appreciation. You know, Jasper didn't do *everything*. I'm the one who rented the truck, and got the fertilizer.
SARAH. You want a gift? Here - I bought you a hat.
DOOLEY. A hat?
SARAH. For a disguise.

(She hands him a fishing hat.)

DOOLEY. This is an old fart's hat. What, am I going fishing with Henry Fonda?
SARAH. You don't want to get picked up by the cameras.
DOOLEY. I already have a disguise, thank you.

(DOOLEY puts on a baseball cap with a blonde wig attached to it, and dons sunglasses.)

SARAH. *(Laughs.)* Oh, that's great. You don't look the least bit suspicious.
DOOLEY. It's better than sailing on Golden Pond.
SARAH. *(Shrugs.)* Whatever. It's your ass.
DOOLEY. That's exactly right. I'm taking the big risk, I'll wear any goddamn hat I like.

(Beat. DOOLEY keeps eating. SARAH paces, wandering the room.)

SARAH. Jesus. This is so boring. I wish there was something to do.
DOOLEY. You want to screw around?
SARAH. *(Chuckles.)* Yeah, that's an option. That's what these rooms are for, aren't they? Tawdry middle-class affairs. People stealing away in shame, feeding their empty lives with emptier sex, celebrating the great lie of bourgeois success. I wonder just how many times some fat sweaty corporate executive took a break from raping his investors to drag his big-haired secretary here and poke at her with his nubby little pig dick? All those pillars of the community, the bankers, the lawyers, the CEOs, the whole crew of gut-

less weasels, pleasuring themselves, stealing our money, selling our country down the river...! It's sickening. It's vomitous. I could kill them all and not lose a moment's sleep.

(Beat.)

    DOOLEY. So you want to?

(Points to the bed.)

    SARAH. What, are you crazy?
    DOOLEY. You said you were bored...
    SARAH. You think because I'm bored, I'm gonna sleep with you? I'd have to be completely *un*-bored. I'd have to be so fucking distracted that I didn't care *what* I was doing. I mean, grow up. We don't have time for stupid stuff like that.
    DOOLEY. We don't have time? We've been sitting here doing jackshit for three days. If we'd been having sex all that time, at least we'd be deepening our friendship.
    SARAH. Dream on.
    DOOLEY. Why? Because you're Jasper's girl?
    SARAH. I'm not Jasper's anything.
    DOOLEY. Oh, please. You think I don't have the inside story on you two?
    SARAH. I'm nobody's "girl". I'm a fucking freedom fighter!
    DOOLEY. Yeah, right. I know your type - you're one of those radical groupies, you get off on that whole charismatic-leader bullshit. You won't even look at me, I'm just a fucking foot soldier, but once this thing goes down and my stock shoots sky-high, oh yeah, then you won't be able to keep your hands off me. You'll be all, "Oh, Dooley, that's such a sexy name..."

(DOOLEY illustrates by grabbing at her.)

    SARAH. Hey, fuck off!

(She bats him away, and when he persists, she assumes a defensive karate stance..)

    DOOLEY. Oh, what? You think you can kick my ass?
    SARAH. Only one way to find out.

KIDNEY STONES

DOOLEY. *(As he grudgingly backs off.)* It's just not right. I'm on an important mission here, I have to be at optimal mind-set. I should think if there were some small way you could attend to my needs, get me combat-ready, you would jump at the chance. Apparently not. Apparently I expect too much.

SARAH. Apparently.

DOOLEY. Tell you this, those Arab fanatics, I'll bet they *make* their women service them. It's probably a religious thing with them. That's the trouble with America: nobody goes to church anymore. No sense of discipline. That's why we're in the shitty state we're in today.

SARAH. We're in this shitty state because the government and the industrial complex have formed a capitalistic cabal to screw the ordinary working man and sap the life out of our *Constitution.*

DOOLEY. Exactly. We let these camel-fuckers waltz into the country, give them all the amenities, flying lessons and everything, and then they turn around and shove it right back up our ass. So how do we respond? Okay, granted, we bomb a couple of caves in Afghanistan, but also, we start restricting our own liberties. Airport searches, gun controls, all kinds of totalitarian bullshit. Getting everything ass-backwards. We're the *good* guys. Don't restrict us - restrict *them*! And that's what I'm gonna say in my interview. Oh, I'm gonna lay some scary shit on them. I'm gonna do some serious mind-fucking.

SARAH. What interview?

DOOLEY. You know - with Dan Rather or one of those 60 Minutes guys. Tom Brokaw. Not Peter Jennings - he's a fucking Canadian. We blindfold them and take them to an undisclosed location - maybe here, that would be poetic justice - and I sit in the shadows, electronically disguise my voice... *(Using an "electronic" voice.)* "Remember Waco! Remember Ruby Ridge...!" It's gonna be so cool.

SARAH. This is not about individual self-promotion, you know.

DOOLEY. Hey, every movement needs a poster boy, so why not me? I'm gonna have this whole outlaw mystique going. Like some rock star, or James Dean. I'll be getting all kinds of pussy, oh yeah.

SARAH. You're a weird fuck, aren't you?

DOOLEY. Only one way to find out.

(PHONE RINGS. DOOLEY reaches for phone..)

SARAH. Don't answer it! Wait for the second ring.

KIDNEY STONES

(DOOLEY doesn't answer. There is a second RING, and then silence.)

SARAH. *(Nods.)* Okay - that was them.
DOOLEY. Good thing we didn't answer.
SARAH. They'll call back.

(SARAH stands over the phone, waiting.)

DOOLEY. This is one stupid fucking system. Really inspires confidence in the leadership.
SARAH. Hey, you've been spouting a lot of reactionary shit lately. Are you down with the cause or not?
DOOLEY. I'm down with the cause. I'm just not down with Jasper, like some of us.
SARAH. You better watch what you say. When the revolution comes, you don't want to be on the wrong side.
DOOLEY. Hey, I *am* the revolution, baby...!

(PHONE RINGS again.)

SARAH. Shh! *(She answers phone.)* Falcon here.
DOOLEY. *(Scornful.)* Falcon...
SARAH. *(Into phone.)* Yes...The moon is in the seventh house. Is the heather on the hill?... *(SARAH looks at DOOLEY, and nods her head, "It's them" DOOLEY gives a sarcastic thumbs-up.)* Yes, we're ready for further instructions. Please advise...What? There's a partridge in the pear tree? *(Confused.)* What does that mean?...Really? Oh wow. No shit.
DOOLEY. What? What?
SARAH. *(Into phone.)* Yeah, I see...So what do we do?...Uh huh...Uh huh...
DOOLEY. What?
SARAH. Well - you want to talk to him yourself?... *(DOOLEY reaches for the phone, but SARAH doesn't offer it.)* Oh. Okay. No, I understand. We have to adjust...Well, it is what it is...Yeah, okay. Roger, over and out.

(Hangs up.)

DOOLEY. Are you gonna tell me what, or what?
SARAH. Change in plans.
DOOLEY. What?

KIDNEY STONES

SARAH. The drop is off.

DOOLEY. The drop is off?

SARAH. Something must have leaked. All of a sudden they have guards set up, surveillance cameras...It's a whole new deal.

DOOLEY. Shit! See? You see? We should have done it last week! I told them! But no, we have to wait! Fucking pussies! All this James Bond bullshit with phone messages and code names, and now the whole mission is fucked!

SARAH. It's not fucked. The mission is still on.

DOOLEY. Yeah, right, we're just gonna improvise something now, after all that meticulous planning? Burns my ass! Wasting our time sitting around in this dump - no cupcakes...! Ahh...! *(With resignation.)* You know what? Whatever. They're running the show. Whatever they say. New plan? Why not? Let's hear the new plan. I'm sure it's good. Jasper came up with it, so it must be fucking brilliant. Let's hear the brilliant new plan.

SARAH. *(Deep breath.)* Okay, well...It appears we're gonna have to crash the gate.

DOOLEY. *(Scoffs.)* Yeah, right.

SARAH. *(Serious.)* No, right.

DOOLEY. We're gonna crash the gate?

SARAH. Well, you. You're gonna.

DOOLEY. *I'm* gonna?

SARAH. You're the driver.

DOOLEY. So I'm gonna crash the gate, and then what?

SARAH. And then set off the bomb.

DOOLEY. Set it off with what?

SARAH. With a button-I don't know. You're the Munitions Expert.

DOOLEY. So I set off the bomb, and then what?

SARAH. And then the bomb goes off. I think that's the logical progression.

(Beat.)

DOOLEY. Let's go over this, so I can get it clear in my mind: I'm in the truck, and the bomb's in the truck, and I crash the gate, and I set off the bomb...There's a crucial step missing here. Mainly, what the fuck happens to *me?*

(Long beat..)

SARAH. See, the mission has *changed.*

KIDNEY STONES

DOOLEY. *(Understands.)* Now it's a suicide mission.
SARAH. Uh huh.
DOOLEY. And I'm the suicide.
SARAH. Uh huh.
DOOLEY. So I'm dead.
SARAH. Basically.

(Beat.)

DOOLEY. Gotta say, that's a little harsh.
SARAH. It's a regrettable development, to be sure.
DOOLEY. I really didn't sign up for that!
SARAH. You pledged yourself to the cause, didn't you?
DOOLEY. The cause won't do me any good if I'm dead.
SARAH. Sometimes we have to make sacrifices for the sake of our guiding principles.
DOOLEY. My biggest guiding principle is staying alive, and I can tell you right now, I'm willing to sacrifice *anything* to preserve that.
SARAH. Unfortunately that's not an option. The fight for liberty, as history teaches us, is a stark and bloody one. We're trying to reclaim our birthright as a free people here, and if we have to pay the ultimate price to secure that freedom, then so be it.
DOOLEY. So why don't you do it?
SARAH. I can't drive a stick.
DOOLEY. I'll teach you. It's not that fucking hard.
SARAH. Look, they want *you* to do it. Those are the orders.
DOOLEY. They can go fuck themselves. I'm not getting myself blown up into a million pieces for their amusement, no way.
SARAH. *(Brightly.)* Maybe you won't get blown up. I mean, with all those guards, you might actually be shot dead before you even reach the gate.
DOOLEY. Oh, I didn't realize there was a silver lining.
SARAH. It's definitely a tough break, but what are you gonna do?
DOOLEY. What am *I* gonna do? I'm gonna pack my things and get the fuck out of here.
SARAH. What do you mean?
DOOLEY. I mean I'm booking. I'm out.
SARAH. You can't be out.
DOOLEY. *(Packing his things.)* Sorry, but this isn't my thing. I don't want to kill a lot of innocent people.
SARAH. You didn't mind killing them before.

KIDNEY STONES

DOOLEY. That was different. That was a surgical strike against a symbol of oppression - there was nothing personal about it. This way - driving right up to a crowd of people, just standing there drinking their coffee - that's vicious, man. It's like playing God, and I'm not into that scene.

SARAH. I think you're just afraid to die.

DOOLEY. Bin-go! I'm not one of those Al Qaeda wackos, thinks he's gonna spend eternity in paradise screwing a bunch of virgins. I want my reward now, on earth, thank you.

SARAH. Well, I gotta say, I'm a little disappointed in your attitude, Dooley.

DOOLEY. *(As he gathers the cards on the floor.)* And your approval means so much to me right now.

SARAH. No, I thought you were the real thing. I thought you had real balls.

DOOLEY. Oh, I have real balls. They hang on either side of my dick, and that's where I plan to keep them. I like that arrangement.

SARAH. This is such a great opportunity for you. You're gonna become a legend, do you realize that? This is your dream. They'll write folksongs about you, put you on A&E Biography....Just like James Dean.

DOOLEY. I don't really give a fuck about James Dean. I never did.

SARAH. And on a personal note, I'll always be proud to say that I worked with you.

DOOLEY. *(Intrigued.)* Yeah? *(Then he dismisses it.)* Nice try. You and your fucking feminine wiles. This was probably your idea in the first place.

SARAH. You heard me on the phone, I didn't say a word.

DOOLEY. Because it was all in code. "The heather on the hill" and all that shit. You and Jasper, working your little conspiracies, trying to kill me off.

SARAH. Why would we do that?

DOOLEY. Because I'm a threat to the organization. I speak my mind, I challenge authority, and that scares you guys. You want everyone to be a fucking lemming, following orders, and you're afraid some of those lemmings will start following me - the man with the common touch, the true leader.

SARAH. Who's gonna follow you? You don't even have the guts to drive a itty-bitty truck through a tiny little gate.

DOOLEY. I'm an American, and Americans don't commit suicide. That's part of our national character. We fight, we rebel, and we win! Our founding fathers - not one of them took the pipe. Not even Benedict Arnold. So call Lover-boy and tell him to get another stooge, somebody from a foreign coun-

try, where life is cheap. I'm outta here.
SARAH. Dooley, think hard about this: if you make the wrong move, it could haunt you the rest of your life.
DOOLEY. And if I make the right move, the rest of my life will be about two hours long. No thanks. Bring on the ghosts.

(DOOLEY starts for the door, but SARAH blocks him.)

SARAH. We have to complete this mission.
DOOLEY. You complete it. *(Mimics a stick shift.)* Reverse, neutral, drive, second, third. It's like an "H". Piece of cake. *(He hands her the truck keys.)*
SARAH. You can't just walk out like this, Dooley. You have an obligation.
DOOLEY. I didn't sign any contract. This was a labor of love for me, and frankly the love is gone.
SARAH. Then you'd better try to fake it. Or else.
DOOLEY. Or else what? You're gonna revoke my membership?
SARAH. Or else you won't live to tell the tale.
DOOLEY. *(Mockingly.)* I won't live to tell the tale? Are you kidding with that shit..?

(DOOLEY moves towards the door again, and SARAH pulls out a gun.)

DOOLEY. *(A shocked laugh.)* What the fuck...?
SARAH. Okay? So make up your mind.
DOOLEY. You're not gonna shoot me. *(As DOOLEY moves towards her, she jabs the gun at him and he prudently retreats.)* Okay, okay, don't be a fucking hero. *(Beat.)* Can we talk about this?
SARAH. Nothing to talk about. I have my orders.
DOOLEY. You have orders to get rid of me? That fucking Jasper...!
SARAH. You can't back out of a mission. That's not an option.
DOOLEY. So my choices are, kill myself or be killed. This is your idea of freedom? *(Shakes his head.)* I knew I shouldn't have got involved with you people. Should have gone out on my own, been a lone vigilante, a sniper or something. Fucking organizations are all the same. I joined the Boy Scouts when I was a kid, and that was bullshit, too. So political. *(Beat.)* That's a nice gun. Where'd you get it?
SARAH. Peabody's Gun and Ammo. Floor model.
DOOLEY. Can I see it? *(SARAH just stares at him.)* There's something fucked up in this country when somebody can own a gun, but she can't drive

KIDNEY STONES

a stick shift.
SARAH. What's it gonna be, Dooley?

(Beat.)

DOOLEY. Well, I'm not gonna let some girl shoot me. *(He puts his things down.)* Might as well go out in a blaze of glory. Start building the legend.
SARAH. *(Lowers the gun.)* All right then. They change shifts at 1530 - that's 3:30 - so there'll be lots of activity and confusion. More people, more potential collateral damage, bigger media exposure - hopefully they'll pre-empt Oprah. It takes about twenty minutes to make the trip, so we have about half-an-hour to prepare. You'd better rig up the truck.
DOOLEY. That'll take two seconds. Maybe I'll go out and get myself a last meal. Cupcakes, hopefully. *(As SARAH follows him to the door.)* You don't have to come with me.
SARAH. Yes I do.
DOOLEY. You don't trust me? Jesus. You'd think, being a martyr, I'd get a little more respect. What are you gonna do, hold that gun on me right up to the moment we explode?
SARAH. I guess so.
DOOLEY. *(Realizes she's serious.)* What, are you crazy?
SARAH. You have a job, I have a job.
DOOLEY. Don't be fucking stupid. Stay out of it.
SARAH. I can't, now.
DOOLEY. What's the sense in both of us getting killed? Look, Sarah - I promise, I'll go through with the mission. I'll blow myself up. I'm starting to look forward to it. But you have to live. Who's gonna tell my story to the world? Who's gonna do my 60 Minutes interview?
SARAH. We're a team. We go down together.

(Beat.)

DOOLEY. *(Sighs with resignation.)* Fucking fanatics. Nothing but trouble.
SARAH. *(With growing enthusiasm.)* This is a great day, Dooley. We're going to wake up the world. This country is dry and withered, and ready to burn. All we have to do is light the match. The moment is here, the moment is now. *(Waving her gun high.).* Thirty minutes to Armageddon! All aboard!
DOOLEY. So you want to screw around before we go? You gotta be pretty fucking distracted by now. *(SARAH glares at him.)* You know, Sarah,

KIDNEY STONES

you're probably a very good revolutionary, but you're kinda cold on the personal level.
    SARAH. I'm focused. I'm committed. That's why I joined the organization. I'm not sure why you joined.
    DOOLEY. Frankly I was hoping to meet women.
    SARAH. And you met me.
    DOOLEY. Yeah. Ha. *(Shrugs.)* Well - nothing left to do but wait, I guess.
    SARAH. I guess.

(DOOLEY picks up the deck of cards. He sits, and starts flipping the cards into the wastebasket. SARAH pulls up a chair beside him, and watches. DOOLEY cuts the deck, and hands half to SARAH. They both sit back and flip cards into the wastebasket.)

KIDNEY STONES

COSTUME PLOT

DOOLEY
Army fatigue jacket
T-shirt
Dark blue work pants
Work boots

SARAH
Blue jeans
Sweater
Light coat
Beret

PROPERTY PLOT

Deck of cards
Fishing hat
Baseball cap with fake hair attached
Bag of groceries:
Sandwiches
Twizzlers
Gatorade
Crunchy Cheetos
Fruit cocktail
Apples
Devil Dogs
Gun
Phone

KIDNEY STONES

HARVEST TIME

(A bedroom. MIKE sits up in bed, hooked up to a dialysis machine, as he watches TV. His brother BILLY ENTERS.)

BILLY. Yo! Mikey!
MIKE. *(Dully.)* Billy.
BILLY. *(Jokingly.)* Don't get up. *(MIKE is unamused.)* Whatcha doin', bro?
MIKE. What does it look like I'm doing? I'm hooked up to this fucking machine.
BILLY. *(Checks out the machine.)* Man, look out all these dials. Is that where they get that word, "dialysis"? "Dials"?
MIKE. Don't touch it, okay.
BILLY. So your blood is like going in and out of your body even as we speak, right? That's pretty cool. *(BILLY sits in a chair.)* What are we watching here? *Golf?*
MIKE. I'll watch any fucking thing these days.
BILLY. NASCAR's on, you know.
MIKE. I'm not watching NASCAR.
BILLY. You don't like NASCAR? NASCAR's great.
MIKE. Yeah, I'm gonna sit here like a jerk-off and watch a bunch of rednecks drive their cars in a circle for two hours.
BILLY. Better than watching these country club assholes walking around in the grass swinging their sticks. That ain't no sport. There's no danger involved. Even in tennis, you know, you could rip your tendon or something. But this is bullshit.
MIKE. It's Zen, Billy. Golf is a Zen thing. You hit the ball, it goes up in the air, it comes down...It's very pure.

(AMY, Mike's wife, ENTERS.)

AMY. Hi, Billy.
BILLY. Hey, Amy.
AMY. You want something to drink? Beer? Wine cooler?
BILLY. You got any hard lemonade?
AMY. No.
BILLY. Beer.

(AMY EXITS.)

BILLY. I've been drinking a lot of that hard lemonade lately. Nice change of pace.

MIKE. Not drinking too much, I hope?
BILLY. I'm always in control.
MIKE. 'Cause you gotta take care of that kidney.
BILLY. Oh. Yeah.
MIKE. It's almost time to harvest, you know.
BILLY. Harvest?
MIKE. You know.
BILLY. Oh. Yeah. *(Beat.)* I thought you were good for another year.
MIKE. Fucking thing is disintegrating. That's why I'm on this machine every other day. Doctor Zinkovich thinks we might have to do it next month.
BILLY. Next month? Huh!
MIKE. Which they say is a simple procedure. Cut it out, stick it in. Only takes a couple of weeks to recover. It's not like you're working, anyway. You can watch all the NASCAR you want.
BILLY. Sounds great.

(AMY returns with a can of beer.)

AMY. Here you go.
BILLY. Thanks, Ame.
AMY. You're welcome. Mike, you want anything?
MIKE. What am I gonna want?
AMY. I'm just asking.
MIKE. No.
AMY. Beer? Wine cooler?
MIKE. No.
AMY. You sure?
MIKE. I said no.
BILLY. How about some hard lemonade?
AMY. You want hard lemonade?
MIKE. Do we *have* any hard lemonade?
AMY. No, but I can get you some.
MIKE. I don't want any!
AMY. You sure?
MIKE. Yes!

(AMY rolls her eyes at BILLY with resigned amusement, and EXITS.)

BILLY. She's sweet.

KIDNEY STONES

MIKE. Drives me fucking crazy. She knows when I'm on the machine, I got no patience. She does it on purpose.
BILLY. You don't appreciate the love of a good woman.
MIKE. Yeah, wait till you have the love of a good woman. You ain't gonna appreciate it, either.
BILLY. So let me ask you a personal question: does this, with all the medication and everything, does this interfere with, you know, you and Amy...um...doing whatever?
MIKE. What kind of shit is that to ask?
BILLY. I said it was a personal question.
MIKE. It's none of your fucking business!
BILLY. Fair enough.
MIKE. *(Shaking his head.)* Jesus...!
BILLY. No, I respect that. The privacy of marriage. But I think it's a shame we can't talk about such things, you and me, because of our maleness. Because women get together, they can talk about *anything*. You ever watch that Sex in the City? Jesus Christ! They're talking about uncircumsized dicks and cervical mucous and every fucking thing. And I'll tell you a secret, I wouldn't sleep with any one of them. They think they're so fucking hot? Not in my book.
MIKE. *(Watching TV.)* Look at this shot. He had to go over the tree, and now it's coming in pin-high...Look, i-i-it's... oh! Lipped the cup! Jesus, that was beautiful. See what I mean, Billy? Zen! It's a beautiful thing.
BILLY. Can I check NASCAR for a minute?
MIKE. No, you can't check NASCAR!
BILLY. Come on. This guy's up by four strokes. Just to check...

(He reaches for the remote..)

MIKE. Hey, what is wrong with you, Billy? I'm sick here, I'm getting my blood cleaned in front of your eyes, and all you care about is NASCAR? How about a little fucking sympathy, please? Is that too much to ask? What is there to *check*, anyway? The cars go around and around and around - it's *meaningless*.
BILLY. It's not meaningless. Some of those cars are going two hundred miles an hour.
MIKE. Going *where?* Where are they going? In a fucking circle! Think about that! I mean, get a *life!*

(Beat.)

KIDNEY STONES

BILLY. Somebody's on the rag today.

MIKE. Between the two of you - NASCAR, hard lemonade...Jesus! *(Takes a deep breath.)* You're right. I shouldn't take this out on you. You're the only one who's coming through for me.

BILLY. *(Shrugs.)* Hey.

MIKE. And don't think I'm non-appreciative. Don't think I'm an ungrateful scumbag, because I'm not. I may not express myself, but you know how I feel.

BILLY. Sure.

MIKE. What happens is - you sit around all day, and you start to think. You have no choice. And you get philosophical. Because your whole life, it all boils down to one shitty little organ in your body you never gave a second thought. And now it's running the whole show. And everything gets turned upside-down. I mean, you're my younger brother, I shouldn't be needing your help. I should be giving you *my* kidney. And I would, I would give you my kidney, if it wasn't all fucked up.

BILLY. I know you would, man.

MIKE. Or an eye, or an arm, or whatever. I'll tell you something, once this operation goes through and I'm back on my feet, I'm gonna do a lotta things different. I'm not gonna waste my life anymore. Because time is precious. That's something you learn. *(Takes BILLY's arm.)* And I'm gonna take care of you, Billy, because you took care of me, and I don't forget. This whole thing, maybe it was a blessing. You and me, we could have gone on forever, all our lives, without having our bonds of brotherhood tested. We never would have known what we've got here, this special thing, this precious - thing... *(Starting to lose it.)* Thank God for you, Billy. I say it every day - Thank God, thank God...

(MIKE starts to cry, and looks away, covering his face. BILLY is respectfully quiet for a moment, and then he stealthily reaches for the remote. As AMY enters with a cordless phone, BILLY sits back quickly.)

AMY. Mike - your mother's on the phone. Mike?

MIKE. *(Tightly.)* Can't talk now.

AMY. Are you okay?

MIKE. I just can't talk! Okay?

AMY. *(Offers the phone.)* Billy?

BILLY. *(Waves her off, whispers.)* I'm not here.

AMY. *(Back to phone.)* Mom? - No , Mike is asleep...No, he's fine...

KIDNEY STONES

(AMY EXITS, as MIKE recovers his composure.)

BILLY. Ma thinks I'm driving the cab. Don't wanna disillusion her.
MIKE. Billy, Billy...when are you gonna get a real job? There must be something you can do. Seriously, if this transplant doesn't work and I wind up croaking, what are you gonna do? I want you to think about your future.
BILLY. Don't worry. Something always happens to me. *(Beat.)* Actually, I was gonna mention - I got another offer.
MIKE. Really? Well, see, that's good. That's a start. *(Beat.)* Another offer for what?
BILLY. My kidney.
MIKE. Another offer?
BILLY. Yeah. Some guy. Wants it for his son.
MIKE. Somebody else wants your kidney?
BILLY. Uh huh.
MIKE. Well - how the fuck did that come about?
BILLY. *(Shrugs.)* I don't know. The kid needs a transplant for some reason. I didn't inquire into the specifics. None of my business, really.
MIKE. No, I mean, how did it come about that this guy wants *your* kidney? You're just making conversation or something, and he suddenly says, "Hey, I want your kidney?"
BILLY. No, he saw it on the Internet, I assume.
MIKE. The Internet?
BILLY. Yeah. I put it on e-Bay, and he musta seen it.
MIKE. You put my kidney on e-Bay?
BILLY. *(Corrects him.)* My kidney.
MIKE. *(Clarifying.)* The kidney you're giving me?
BILLY. Well, since I was losing it anyway, I thought I'd see how much it was worth. Just to satisfy my curiosity. *(Brightly.)* It's worth a lot.
MIKE. You know, that's against the law, asshole. You can't sell organs on the internet.
BILLY. Sure, you can. You just have to be a little creative. I called it a "urine filtration system". I've always been good with words, you know that.
MIKE. And what did this guy offer?
BILLY. Fifty thousand.
MIKE. Fifty thousand? Shit!
BILLY. It should be more, right?
MIKE. Well, I would *think*. I mean, it's a valuable piece of your body. You can't just grow another one.
BILLY. That's what I figured, so I got him up to seventy-five. Hey, the

KIDNEY STONES

guy's a millionaire, he can afford that much for his kid, I hope.
MIKE. So wait a minute - you actively negotiated with him?
BILLY. That's part of the fun.
MIKE. Isn't he gonna be pissed off when you don't go through with it?
BILLY. What do you mean?
MIKE. I mean...when you don't...because you're not...because...

(BILLY looks away evasively. Beat.)

MIKE. Billy - you promised me that kidney.
BILLY. I didn't *promise*...
MIKE. You fucking promised!
BILLY. *(Patiently.)* I said I would give you my kidney. And I *would*, if I could spare it. But seventy-five thousand...man, that would really clear up my financial situation in a heartbeat, you know?
MIKE. What are you talking about? I had first dibs on that kidney, Billy. I'm your brother!
BILLY. I'm aware of that, Michael. And if I had only one kidney, I would gladly give it to you, because you *are* my brother, and I'd be more than happy to sacrifice my life for yours. But I have *two* kidneys, see, which totally changes the equation. Now it becomes a business thing: I own this commodity, which I can only sell once, and it's my personal responsibility to get full market value. You can see that..*(MIKE doesn't see it. BILLY points towards TV.)* It's like, okay, Tiger Woods - suppose he finds out he's got this new disease, and if he swings a golf club too many times he can become crippled for life?
MIKE. What kind of fucking disease is that?
BILLY. It's a hypothetical disease - bear with me. Okay, so he's got like one golf game left in him. Do you think he's gonna play it for free? Go out with his buddies to Eisenhower Park or something, bring along a six-pack, make five-dollar bets on the longest drive? No, he's gonna go to CBS or HBO and set up the biggest payday he can find, ten or twenty million - Thanksgiving Day, promotions with Nike and all that shit - because that's what you gotta do - maximize your earning potential. Some people will say he's a greedy fuck, but I say no, he's just doing right by himself, which is why we're all here, let's face it. It's not Zen anymore, it's business.
MIKE. That's a stupid fucking analogy, okay? That's sports, and this is life-and-death.
BILLY. All the more reason. Look at my man Dale Earnhardt; he's cruising along at Daytona, king of the world, next thing you know he's dead.

KIDNEY STONES

Dead in four-tenths of a second.

MIKE. And the point there is...?

BILLY. You can be gone before you know it. And I don't want to die with two good unused kidneys just rotting inside me. I want to harvest every asset I have, while it's still viable. Because someday all too soon they're gonna have artificial kidneys. The market will dry up. Gotta strike now, Mikey. Gotta maximize my earning potential - simple as that.

MIKE. *(Smiles.)* You're breaking my balls, right? You gotta be breaking my balls. 'Cause you'd have to be a monumental prick to promise your own brother, *your own brother*, a life-saving kidney, and then sell it right out from under him. You'd have to be a prick among pricks, and regardless of your past history, I can't believe you would sink that low.

BILLY. I don't think you're looking at the big picture here, Mikey.

MIKE. The big picture is I'm fucking dying! I don't have a hypothetical disease! *That's* the big picture!

BILLY. That's *your* big picture. See, your trouble is, ever since you got this kidney failure thing, you've become very self-absorbed. You should walk a mile in my moccasins for a change. You're always saying I should get a job? Well, this guy has a big estate on the North Shore, and guess who he wants to be the caretaker?

MIKE. You?

BILLY. *(Nods decisively.)* The man who takes care of things. I'll have my own little house on the property - which is called the caretaker's house - and I'll wear a little cap, and I'll have a little U-haul with all my tools in it. Hedge-clippers and shit. Plus, benefits. Oh, it's a sweet deal. And I've always loved nature, you know that.

MIKE. *(Skeptical.)* Yeah, this guy's gonna let you be a caretaker with only one kidney? Come on! He's jerking your chain.

BILLY. For seventy-five grand he can jerk whatever he wants.

MIKE. Fuck the seventy-five grand, Billy! I'm your brother!

BILLY. You keep saying you're my brother. Hey, I'm *your* brother. Shouldn't you be a little happy for me, I got a chance to turn my life around? You're never supportive.

MIKE. And what's supposed to happen to *my* life now? This certainly puts me up shit's creek, doesn't it?

BILLY. Granted, there's a down side. But with all the people in the world out there, all the spare kidneys, I gotta believe something's gonna work out for you. You can never stop hoping; I found that out.

MIKE. *(Shakes his head.)* You really fooled me, Billy. I thought this time you'd finally changed. Finally managed to turn yourself into a human being.

KIDNEY STONES

But no, you're the same old Billy, same lying sneaking little rat bastard. You've always got some scam going, don't you? Well, this one's gonna backfire on you just like all the others, but I won't be around to help you this time because I'll be dead.

BILLY. This is why I hate coming here. You're always so fucking negative.

MIKE. You promised me, Billy!

BILLY. Promised, promised...! You promised me you'd give me your Tom Seaver 1967 rookie card, didn't you? Didn't you? Instead you gave it to Danny Morley, "your best friend in the world", who wound up stealing Allison Steinberg right out from under your dick. Remember that? All right, you reneged, you fucked me over - do you hear me crying about it? Do you hear me harboring resentment? No - I go forward. You can't live in the past.

MIKE. So that's it, Billy - you're abandoning me? You're just gonna let me waste away?

BILLY. That's the wrong way to look at it. I'm helping a little kid experience a full rich life. Let's not forget the little kid in this.

MIKE. If I can't depend on you - if I can't depend on my own family - my own blood - Shit, why go on living anyway? What's the point? What's the fucking point...?

(MIKE starts to cry, turns away.)

BILLY. Jesus, you're crying again? *(BILLY reaches out to comfort him.)* Come on, Mike, it's gonna be all right...

MIKE. *(Suddenly grabs him by the shirt.)* You miserable son-of-a-bitch!

(He shakes him violently.)

BILLY. Look out - I'm spilling my beer...!

MIKE. You promised me that kidney, you fuck, and I'm taking it!

(BILLY wrests himself out of MIKE's grip and backs away.)

BILLY. Yeah? What are you gonna do? You gonna cut it out or something? *(Calls offstage.)* Hey, Amy, could you bring us a steak knife, please?

AMY. *(Offstage.)* What?

BILLY. *(Pulls up his shirt.)* Which one you want? Right one, left one?

MIKE. *(Disgusted.)* Just get the fuck away from me.

BILLY. Hey, you're the one who said I should look out for myself, in case the transplant don't work.

MIKE. It's definitely not gonna work without a kidney!

BILLY. You gotta stop feeling sorry for yourself. Listen, I didn't make any deal yet. The kidney is still up for grabs. I'm willing to listen to any offer.

MIKE. Gee, isn't that great? Here I am, I got no money, I'm on the balls of my ass - What am I gonna offer you?

(AMY ENTERS.)

AMY. Did you want something? *(Sees the spilt beer.)* Oops. Somebody made a little mess.

(AMY grabs a towel, and bends down to clean up the spill. BILLY watches her admiringly, and then looks significantly at MIKE. MIKE understands. He is appalled. AMY rises, and sees them trading looks.)

AMY. What are you two cooking up? You're a couple of devils. Billy, are you staying for dinner? We've got London broil.

BILLY. Count me in.

(AMY EXITS.)

MIKE. You gotta be kidding.

BILLY. It's something for both of us to consider.

MIKE. You just crossed the line, do you realize that? I mean, you're going to Hell just for thinking that. Just for entertaining the thought. Have a good trip. Give my regards to Satan.

BILLY. I'm just saying, it's a way around the money situation. It's like bartering. If we were a couple of Native Americans, this is what we would do.

MIKE. Un-fucking-believable. You're exploiting me, Billy. I'm a helpless victim, and you're outright raping me.

BILLY. This again is a matter of perspective. I don't feel that I'm raping anybody - I'm providing a service, and I'm getting a service in return. I have a kidney I can't use, you have a wife you can't use. It's quid quo pro, like in <u>Silence of the Lambs.</u>

MIKE. Fucking me right up the ass...! And after all I've done for you! All the money I loaned you - gave you! - I never saw a penny of it again...!

BILLY. Yeah, all the money, but let's face it, there was always some hitch. "Here's ten bucks, but you have to wash my car." "Here's a fifty, but you have to bring my plates down to the Motor Vehicle Bureau." Always some demeaning, degrading little errand...rubbing my nose in it that I was a fuck-up. So now the shoe's on *my* foot. Hey, I know what it's like to be a victim. It's no fun. But that's the way it goes.

MIKE. You know, she's not gonna sleep with you.

BILLY. Oh no? Why not?

MIKE. Because she thinks you're a shithead.

BILLY. She's never expressed that opinion to me.

MIKE. She's never expressed it to you because she's a nice person, but in private, she has more than once made the observation. A *stupid* shithead, to quote her exact words.

BILLY. I don't believe it. I think maybe you called me a shithead, and she agreed with you to keep peace in the house. Because she's always had a little thing for me, you know that. There's always been that sexual tension between us, which I never acted on out of respect for our family ties. Did you hear the way she asked me about the London broil? Very flirtatious.

MIKE. You're living in a fucking dementia world. I'm telling you, it's not gonna happen.

BILLY. Well, it would be nice for you if it did. You might present the offer to her in those terms.

MIKE. So let me get this straight - you'd give up seventy-five grand and a steady job just so you could screw my wife?

BILLY. On a regular basis - yes.

MIKE. See, this is why you'll never get your shit together. That is the stupidest fucking deal I've ever heard of. It's like Jack and the Beanstalk or something. I mean, *I'd* take the seventy-five grand.

BILLY. Because you don't appreciate Amy.

MIKE. And you don't appreciate - *(Stops, as he has a new thought.)* What *is* this guy's name, anyway? The millionaire? You never said.

BILLY. Uh...Herman.

MIKE. Herman what?

BILLY. That's his last name. Cornelius Herman.

MIKE. Cornelius, huh? Cornelius Herman? You know what I think? I don't think there is any millionaire. I think you made this whole thing up so you could shake me down.

BILLY. What, you're calling me a liar?

MIKE. I'm calling you an opportunistic fuck. You're using a chronic debilitating disease to weasel your way into my wife's pants. That's pretty pathetic, even for you.

BILLY. If you're gonna be insulting, then forget it. You can't have my

KIDNEY STONES

kidney now.

MIKE. I don't want your kidney! Give it to the fucking kid. Be a big hero.

BILLY. All right, I will! I don't need this bullshit.

MIKE. Good! Go! Get the fuck out!

BILLY. You know, I could just wait till you die, and then sleep with her anyway!

MIKE. She thinks you're a shithead!

BILLY. She does not!

(AMY ENTERS, carrying a beer.)

AMY. Hey! What's all the shouting and carrying on about? *(To MIKE)* You're not supposed to get excited. You're on dialysis.

MIKE. This idiot over here wants to -*(Covering.)* - watch NASCAR...!

AMY. So, he can watch NASCAR for a few minutes, can't he? You have to learn to share. *(Hands BILLY the beer.)* I brought you a fresh beer.

BILLY. Thanks, but I gotta get going...

AMY. You said you were staying for dinner.

BILLY. I know, but...

AMY. Oh, please. There's nothing nicer than a family dinner. And we have a case of beer in the fridge.

BILLY. I don't want to start drinking. I have to drive...

AMY. You can sleep over. There's plenty of room.

BILLY. Well...I guess I could stay...

AMY. Of course you can. Now you two behave. This is no way for brothers to act.

(AMY EXITS. BILLY and MIKE are silent a moment.)

BILLY. Did you hear her voice? She said I could sleep over.

MIKE. She was being nice.

BILLY. *(Nods.)* Yeah. She's a nice kid. Deserves better than you.

MIKE. Maybe so.

(Beat.)

BILLY. Look...About the kidney...I don't know what I'm gonna do. Maybe we can work something out.

MIKE. *(Chuckles.)* Yeah, I can wash your car.

BILLY. You're my brother. You should have whatever organs you need. I don't even know this little kid. He's gonna be walking around with my kidney, this little rich kid punk? I don't think so. I mean, fuck him, you know?
MIKE. *(Sighs.)* Do what you gotta do, Billy. We all gotta do what we gotta do.
BILLY. That's very true, Mike. Very Zen.

(Beat.)

MIKE. *(Wistful.)* Allison Steinberg... Man!
BILLY. She was hot, huh?
MIKE. She was a fox.
BILLY. I saw her the other day at Stop 'N Shop.
MIKE. Yeah? How does she look?
BILLY. She looks good. Well, she's still got that wart.
MIKE. I liked the wart. It worked for her.
BILLY. She was hot.
MIKE. *(With contempt.)* Danny Morley...!
BILLY. Weasel.
MIKE. Rat bastard.

(Beat.)

BILLY. Let's put on NASCAR.
MIKE. Fuck you.

(Blackout..)

KIDNEY STONES

COSTUME PLOT

MIKE
Flannel bathrobe
Pajamas
Slippers

BILLY
Blue jeans
Sneakers
NY Mets t-shirt

AMY
Jeans or stretch slacks
Casual shirt or sweatshirt

PROPERTY PLOT

Dialysis machine
TV Remote control
Television set
Beer cans (2)

SHORT PLAYS FOR EVERY VENUE

JUDGMENT CALL AND OTHER PLAYS
Frederick Stroppel
This collection of darkly comic one-acts by the author of *Single and Proud and Other Plays* includes *Judgment Call, Soulmates, Chain Mail, Perfect Pitch* and *Coelacanth*. (#12658)

ISRAEL HOROVITZ: 5 SHORT PLAYS
Free Gift, Speaking Well of the Dead, Three Weeks After Paradise, Security and *A Mother's Love*, five dramas written in the aftermath of September 11th, are included this collection by the prolific American playwright. (#21973)

OFF-OFF BROADWAY FESTIVAL PLAYS / 27
Born to Be Blue by Mark Bellusci, *The Parrot* by Le Wilhelm, *Flights* by Susan Cameron, *A Doctor's Visit* by Mark Loewenstern, *Three Questions* by Maurice Martin and *The Devil's Parole* by Eric Giancoli were winners in the 27th Annual Short Play Festival. (#17706)

THE KUKKURRIK FABLES
Oscar Mandel
Forty-two playlets for two to ten actors combine wisdom and whimsy for auditions, show fillers or full evenings of Aesop-like tales with a modern twist. (#13060)

SHADOWBOXING
The Shadowbox Cabaret Theatre
Twenty-two outrageous sketches provide an eclectic mix of comic gems, some of the most successful material ever performed at the renowned Columbus cabaret. (#21461)

TEN-MINUTE PLAYS FROM
ACTORS THEATRE OF LOUISVILLE /Volume 5
Edited by Michael Bigelow Dixon and Michele Volansky
Foreword by Jon Jory
Twenty-five short plays by some of the most exciting dramatists writing today are included in this volume. The series is popular for classes and showcases. (#22275)

For the broadest selection of short plays in print, see
THE BASIC CATALOGUE OF PLAYS AND MUSICALS
online at www.samuelfrench.com

DATE DUE	
GAYLORD	PRINTED IN U.S.A.

Samuel French Theater Bookshops

Specializing in plays and books on theater

45 West 25th Street
Second Floor
New York, NY 10010-2751
212 206 8990/FAX 212 206 1429

7623 Sunset Boulevard
Hollywood, CA 90046-2795
323 876 0570/FAX 323 876 6822

11963 Ventura Boulevard
Studio City, CA 91604-2607
818 762 0535

100 Lombard Street (Lower Level)
Toronto, Ontario M5C 1M3
CANADA
416 363 3536
FAX 416 636 1108

52 Fitzroy Street
London W1T 5JR
ENGLAND
011 44 20 7387 9373
FAX 011 44 20 7387 2161

e-mail: samuelfrench@earthlink.net   website: samuelfrench.com

ISBN 0 573 60325 1   #12990